NATIVE FAMILY

# EDWARD S. CURTIS

# NATIVE FAMILY

Christopher Cardozo

PRODUCED BY CALLAWAY EDITIONS

A BULFINCH PRESS BOOK
LITTLE, BROWN AND COMPANY
Boston • New York • Toronto • London

*First Edition*

(COVER)
A FAMILY GROUP – NOATAK, 1928

(FRONTISPIECE)
NEZ PERCÉ BABE, 1900

ISBN 0-8212-2342-9

*Library of Congress Catalog Card Number 96-76438*

*Bulfinch Press is an imprint and trademark of Little, Brown and Company (Inc.)*
*Published simultaneously in Canada by Little, Brown & Company (Canada) Limited*

PRINTED IN HONG KONG

# TABLE OF CONTENTS

# PREFACE

*To the late-twentieth-century eye, the photographs of Native Americans in Edward Sheriff Curtis's* The North American Indian *exhibit a rare empathy as well as a profound intimacy between the photographer and his subject. In the better examples of Curtis's portraits there is a deeply emotional dimension, as well as a degree of romance or the picturesque — a descriptive term frequently used by Curtis himself — communicated within each frame. These qualities, in conjunction with the comprehensive record Curtis created, make his images unique in the history of photography.*

*Curtis's empathetic approach to photographing his subjects is particularly apparent in the images that I consider to be family images: Mothers with their children, brides in traditional nuptial costumes, siblings, elders, home life, and the like, fifty of which are collected here. While the family group as a whole was rarely photographed by Curtis, images relating to family, the idea of home, and family life in general are often found among the thousands of photographs that constitute the visual component of* The North American Indian.

*The unparalleled photographic record that was reproduced in* The North American Indian *was accompanied by a dense, detailed text describing tribal history, traditions, and ways of life. Curtis's written record is organized around twenty-five cardinal points, many of which address issues connected specifically to the notion of family, such as marriage customs, child-rearing, puberty rites, and family structures.*

*Women with their infant children were a favorite subject for Curtis. Many of these images communicate the warmth and tenderness found between a mother and her child, while others appear to be more focused on the diverse clothing, hairstyles, handicrafts, facial types, and physical environments Curtis encountered among the various tribal groups. Thus, the photographs often focus on ethnographic information and issues, rather than the sociology or psychology of tribal families or specific individuals. For instance, emphasis often is placed on clear depictions of an individual's clothing or the construction and decoration of an infant carrying basket. As Curtis explained in his General Introduction: "Rather than being designed for mere embellishment, the photographs are each an illustration of an Indian character or of some vital phase in his existence." However, even in images that were primarily ethnographic in intent, Curtis virtually always attempted to incorporate strong aesthetic elements as well.*

*The idea of family is most powerfully evoked through Curtis's images of children. The youngest members of the various tribes held an obvious fascination for Curtis; there are many images of children among the thousands of photographs he chose to publish in* The North American Indian. *His portraits of Native American children also are among his most moving images, in my view, often displaying a clear spontaneity and a sense of relative ease, with natural poses and happy demeanors. The fact that Curtis was separated from his own children for long periods of time may well have enhanced his fondness for the children he encountered in the field, and engendered the genuinely positive attitude conveyed through his portraits of them.* – C.C.

## FLATHEAD CHILDHOOD, 1910

*The Flatheads controlled that portion of Montana in which lie the valleys of Clarks fork of the Columbia and its tributaries, the Bitterroot (or St. Marys), the Hell Gate, and the Flathead.* Volume VII, page 43.

(OPPOSITE)

## DUCK-SKIN PARKAS, NUNIVAK, 1928

*The most important garment of the Nunivak, and of the Eskimo generally, is the parka. This is a frock, made of animal, bird, or fish skins, which is slipped over the head and reaches about to the knees. The general style for men and women is similar, except that while the bottom hem of the men's garment is regular all the way around, the parka of the woman has a deep slit or open seam on each side, in much the same manner as a white man's shirt. Parkas for outdoor wear, for travelling or hunting, and for winter use, are provided with a hood, which may be drawn up to cover the head, or thrown back at pleasure. Such a hood, made of the same material as the parka itself, usually has a strip of long hair, wolf or wolverene, commonly attached to the edge for ornamentation, so that the wearer, with hood up, seems to have a halo of long hairs outlining his face.* Volume XX, pages 9-10.

(OVERLEAF)

## CAMP BY A PRAIRIE LAKE – PIEGAN, 1911

*Polygyny was the rule, but the first wife was considered the real wife, "she who sits by his side," the others being in a measure servants of the first.* Volume VI, page 13.

## NOATAK CHILD, 1928

*Nearly a week's journey by skin boat up the swift, shallow Noatak river, which empties into the narrow strait connecting Hotham inlet with Kotzebue sound, is situated the winter village of the Noatak people. The little settlement nestles picturesquely in a grove of spruce on a high bluff overlooking the stream, which is wide at this point.*

*These villagers dwell in small log cabins, each containing a single room with bunks built against a side and rear wall. . . .*

*In midwinter some of the most courageous families undertake a truly remarkable journey overland from the Noatak river to the sea and down the coast to Sheshalik in order to arrive in season for the early seal-hunting. Not only is regular equipment for the trail carried, but the hunters haul their large and burdensome umiaks by means of dog-teams. The progress is necessarily slow, involving hunting for food as well as prodigious labor in moving their burdens. The difficulties of the trek are by no means lessened, in the crossing of a mountain range, by the intense cold and the winter storms.* Volume XX, pages 193-194.

(ABOVE)

A CAHUILLA CHILD, 1924

*The beaded cap is as modern as the dress.* Volume XV, page 30.

(OPPOSITE)

CAYUSE MOTHER AND CHILD, 1910

*The Cayuse were a sullen, arrogant, warlike tribe ranging near the Blue mountains in Washington and Oregon, from the head of Touchet river to that of John Day river. . . . The tradition says that these people occupied underground dwellings, which is the only indication of the primitive culture of the Cayuse.* Volume VIII, page 80.

## WHEN WINTER COMES, 1908

*The Sioux were a semi-nomadic people. Through the summer months they moved their camps to follow the buffalo herds, and day after day the hunting parties went out to the killing. Great stores of the meat were cut into thin strips, dried, and pounded into pemmican for use during the winter months when they could not hunt and kill at pleasure. As the autumn closed and the cold northern winds began to sweep across the plains, the hunting parties, large and small, sought the valley of some wood-girt stream, and there in the protection of the forest remained until spring approached. Robes and furs had been brought in for winter bedding and clothing, and were heaped about the tipis in prodigal profusion. Sufficient jerked meat and pemmican had been provided to last them through the winter months, and these, with the stores of berries and roots gathered and prepared by the women, gave promise of a season of plenty. Occasionally a herd of buffalo came within striking distance and gave the men an opportunity for a grand winter hunt. The meat obtained at this season could be kept fresh until warm weather again approached.* Volume III, page 7.

(OPPOSITE)

## GOLDENROD MEADOWS – PIEGAN, 1911

*The deerskin garments customarily worn by plains Indians were used also by the Piegan. Primitively ornamentation was with porcupine-quills and with beads made by perforating the brown-striped seeds of the silverberry. . . . Formerly the hair of both sexes was parted in the middle and hung loosely. . . . Women adopted the style now seen, that of parting the hair in the middle and braiding it at the sides, and men now arrange theirs in the same manner.* Volume VI, page 153.

(OVERLEAF)

## OVERLOOKING THE CAMP – PIEGAN, 1909

*The Piegan (Pikúnni), the Bloods (Kaínôw), and the Blackfeet (Siksiká) are closely related and allied Algonquian tribes, and usually have been designated collectively as Blackfeet. They were formerly forest Indians, and during the early traditional period probably dwelt in the region of Little Slave lake. From this locality, which was doubtless but one of many camping places during their gradual migratory movement from the Atlantic seaboard . . . they moved slowly southward until they reached the buffalo plains of Alberta and Montana and became prairie Indians.* Volume VI, page 3.

## BERRY-PICKERS IN CAMP – CHIPEWYAN, 1926

*The Chipewyan, who call themselves simply Déne ("people"), are a linguistic group occupying the country from Slave river southward to Cold lake, and from Heart lake (55° North, III° 30' West) eastward to Reindeer lake in north-central Saskatchewan. . . .*

*Although vegetal products, and especially roots, were of little importance to the more northerly Chipewyan, the southerly portion of their territory yields a fairly wide variety of such foods, especially four species of* Vaccinium: *blueberries, otter-berries (a species of blueberry on stalks four to six inches high), and dwarf and swamp cranberries; and service-berries, or June-berries* (Amelanchier Canadensis). . . .

*The Chipewyan house was a conical frame of poles covered with caribou-skins. In the southerly territory wrested from the Cree, into which the migratory caribou did not penetrate, moose-skins became the mode.* Volume XVIII, pages 3, 23-24.

## TSAWATENOK GIRL, 1914

*The winter village of the Tsawatenok formerly was Okwunális at the mouth of Kwae [Gwáï], or Kingcome river. The summer locations were along the river. They now spend the winter at Kwaustums . . . on Gilford island, a former Koeksotenok settlement.* Volume X, page 307.

A FAMILY GROUP – NOATAK, 1928

*Villages are composed of small family groups, each headed by the father or grandfather. The nominal ruler of a village is the so-called head-man, one who holds office through superior wisdom, knowledge of ceremonial precept, or shamanistic power.* Volume XX, page 244.

ASSINIBOIN MOTHER AND CHILD, 1926

*The Assiniboin belong to the Siouan stock. The popular name of this tribe is a Chippewa appellation signifying "stone cookers," referring doubtless to the custom of boiling meat with hot stones in bark vessels. . . .*

*The northern Assiniboin used the regulation Plains costume of deerskin clothing – shirt and hip-length leggings for men, dress and knee-length leggings for women, moccasins and robes for both sexes.* Volume XVIII, page 163.

(OPPOSITE)

## A LITTLE OTO, 1927

*In life and manners the Oto compare closely with the other tribes of the western prairies, with all of whom the buffalo was the determining factor. . . .*

*Buffalo and deer furnished hides which were tanned for tipi-covers, costumes, robes, etc.* Volume XIX, pages 151, 226.

(OVERLEAF)

## LODGE INTERIOR – PIEGAN, 1911

*The one distinctive feature of the Piegan lodges is the characteristic decoration of the inner lining. They, like other Indians, often painted their lodges, so as to indicate either the coups of the owner or his medicine, or sometimes both.* Volume VI, page 13.

## FLATHEAD MOTHER, 1910

*The clothing of both sexes was made in the common style of the plains. Much attention was bestowed on the hair. . . . As a rule the women made a braid at each side, doubled it up, and wrapped it with strings of bone beads. They now allow the braids to hang in front of the shoulders. Until about 1845 the custom of wearing a small bone spike or a dentalium shell in the nasal septum was in vogue. . . .*

*Children were named a few days after birth, usually by the father or the grandfather, in the presence of the family and relations. The name chosen was that of some deceased person, either an ancestor or a well-known personage. Since a name was regarded as a part of the individual, it could not be given to a child or assumed by an adult without his permission. A "good name" – one believed to be capable of bringing its bearer good fortune – sometimes was sold for as much as a horse.* Volume VII, pages 72, 75.

(ABOVE)

A COMANCHE CHILD, 1927

(OPPOSITE)

A LITTLE COMANCHE, 1927

*The Comanche are the sole representatives of the Shoshonean stock in Oklahoma. . . . No North American tribe ranged over so broad a territory. . . .*

*Prior to their knowledge of the white race their central habitat was about the headwaters of the Platte river in what is now Wyoming.* Volume XIX, page 181.

## BLACKFOOT COOKERY, 1926

*The prairies of southern Alberta were dominated by three allied Algonquian tribes – Blackfeet, Bloods, and Piegan, composing a part of what is commonly designated the Blackfoot confederacy. . . .*

*In the earliest times of which living traditionists have information the Piegan ranged on Bow river, the Bloods on Red Deer river, the Blackfeet on the Saskatchewan. They gradually worked southward until the Blackfeet were on Bow, the Bloods on Belly, the Piegan on Old Man river and southward to the northern part of what is now Montana. In the summer the three tribes and the Sarsi always camped together for a time.* Volume XVIII, pages xii, 187

(OPPOSITE)

## A PIEGAN PLAY TIPI, 1926

*In life and manners the Piegan differed little from the other purely hunting tribes of the plains region. The buffalo furnished their principal food, and its skin, horns, and bones, with the addition of the skins of antelope, elk, and deer, supplied material for their dwellings, clothing, and implements.* Volume VI, page 11.

(OVERLEAF)

## BOYS IN KAIAK – NUNIVAK, 1928

*The kaiak (kaíyuh) is the most important craft of many of the Alaskan Eskimo, for by means of it the livelihood of the people is chiefly obtained. Men transport themselves from one hunting camp to another in the kaiak; from it they fish, spear waterfowl, and pursue seal and walrus. Almost as soon as a boy can walk, he learns to paddle and manœver this small but efficient craft.* Volume XX, page 12.

*Eskimo boys are trained in manly pursuits from their earliest years and are honored with feasts on taking their first game.* Folio plate 690, Volume XX.

# COAST POMO BRIDAL COSTUME, 1924

*The Pomo are one of the best-known groups of California Indians – a prominence due largely to their residence in a region much employed as playground by the population of the San Francisco Bay cities, and to their highly developed skill in the art of basketry. They controlled fully half of the area of Mendocino, Sonoma, and Lake counties, and a small detached territory in Glenn and Colusa counties. . . .*

*Women wore short, thick kilts of shredded tules, or skirts of deerskin, or, on the coast, shredded redwood-bark. . . . The hair . . . of women was either unconfined or in a knot at the back of the head. . . . Neatly made ear-pendants consisted of magnesite cylinders and feathers, necklaces of discal clam-shell beads and magnesite cylinders. . . .*

*Marriage was arranged by the parents of the young people, but payment for the wife was not discussed. On the appointed day the people assembled in the bride's house, where the youth's father delivered a speech and handed over shell money to the value of twenty-five to fifty dollars. The young couple usually lived for a time with the bride's family and thereafter in the house of the husband's father.* Volume XIV, pages 55, 188, 189.

## A YOUNG YAKIMA, 1910

*At the beginning of the nineteenth century breech-cloth and moccasins were the usual garments for both sexes. About that time began a change which eventually resulted in the adoption of the complete plains style of dress. At the earlier period men cut the hair square in front and did not braid it. Ear-pendants were elk-teeth or dentalium shells, but nose ornaments, according to native information, were not in use. . . .*

*Each of the cognate bands collectively known to us as Yakima was master of the territory where its winter camp was made, and possessed an interest in the common grounds for hunting and fishing, and for gathering berries and roots. Each band had its chief, but in several cases men extended their influence so as practically to control several adjacent and closely related bands.* Volume VII, pages 159, 160.

MATERNITY BELT – APACHE, 1907

*The belt is made from skin of the mountain lion, the black-tail deer, the white-tail deer, and antelope-animals which give birth to their young without trouble. Medicine-men are called in to pray to the spirits of these animals when a woman approaching confinement puts on the belt. It is worn for a day or so only, but constantly during the critical period, not being removed until after the child is born. Prayers are made, first by a mother or father for their daughter, then by a medicine-man, and lastly by the patient to the gods and elements depicted on the belt. These figures are all connected with lightning lines.* Volume I, page 39.

HOPI BRIDAL COSTUME, 1900

*The Hopi are monogamous. An exchange of food between the two interested families is made as a pledge of marriage, and the subsequent wedding rites extend over four days. On the first night the bride's relatives bring her to the house of her prospective husband, where she remains in seclusion three days, grinding meal, which the bridegroom's female relatives make into piki during the fourth night. The next morning is devoted to the wedding feast, and the final act is the washing of the bride's head by her mother-in-law. The couple remain at the husband's home until his relatives have completed the bride's wedding garments, and thereafter reside with her people.* Volume XII, page 221.

# WOMAN'S COSTUME AND BABY SWING – ASSINIBOIN, 1926

*The Assiniboin belong to the Siouan stock. The popular name of this tribe is a Chippewa appellation signifying "stone cookers," referring doubtless to the custom of boiling meat with hot stones in bark vessels. The northern Assiniboin call themselves Yeskábi. . . .*

*The northern Assiniboin used the regulation Plains costume of deerskin clothing . . . dress and knee-length leggings for women, moccasins and robes for both sexes.* Volume XVIII, page 163.

(OPPOSITE)

## WIFE OF HOWLING WOLF – CHEYENNE, 1927

*Marriage was usually arranged by friends of the suitor, who negotiated for the marriage with the woman's family. . . . Polygyny was practised.* Volume XIX, page 225.

(OVERLEAF)

## A HOME IN THE MESQUITE – CHEMEHUEVI, 1924

*The Chemehuevi, in the eastern half of San Bernardino county and the eastern edge of Riverside. . . . house was oblong, and the average size was about ten by twelve feet. Four forked corner posts of mesquite, and one in the middle of each of the shorter sides, were set in the ground to a depth of several feet, and on these were laid three timbers, one connecting each pair of corner posts and the third the two middle ones. . . . The nearly flat roof consisted of dry wormwood stalks* (Artemisia), *laid across the rafters . . . slabs of dry mesquite-bark across the* Artemisia, *green wormwood with the tips directed toward the eaves, a thick covering of fallen mesquite-leaves, and finally a thin layer of earth, which was trampled down compact and smooth. . . .*

*There was no celebration nor dedication of a new dwelling, and the individual built his own house without the assistance of the community. The occupants slept on the floor, and the furnishings were limited to cooking utensils and baskets.* Volume XV, pages 4, 22.

## SISTERS – APSAROKE, 1908

*Young girls had miniature lodges about four feet high, made of buffalo calf-skins, and arranged inside with beds and utensils as in the living lodges. There they played a great deal, pretending to be grown-up women with husbands, much as white children do. On short marches they dragged the small poles for their tipis, and at the end of the day pitched them as did their mothers.*

*The young girl was in the care of her grandmother, who would speak to her in this fashion: "Look at your brothers; they are poor. Try to live so that some one will love you and buy you. When women are taken from their husbands by other men it is not good." Training in household duties began at an early age, and by the time the girl was fourteen she could tan skins and was beginning to make clothing.* Volume IV, page 28-29.

## A HOPI MOTHER, 1921

*Ordinarily the only garments of the primitive Hopi woman were an undyed cotton robe, which passed under the left arm and was fastened above the right shoulder, the edges overlapping at the right side, and an embroidered belt. Arms and lower legs were bare. On special occasions women wore deerskin moccasins, to which were attached white leggings of the same material, each consisting of half of a large skin, which was wrapped round and round the calf like a thick bandage. . . . Calico gowns, moccasins of the Navaho type (except at ceremonies), and blue, footless, woollen stockings in the Zuñi fashion are the favored costume of today.* Volume XII, page 219.

## DRYING MEAT – CHEYENNE, 1927

*As typical Plains Indians, the Cheyenne depended on the buffalo for most of their food supply. The flesh of other animals, deer and antelope chiefly, as well as native fruits, roots, berries, and wild vegetables, were used.* Volume XIX, page 224.

## A BABY APSAROKE, 1908

*If a child misbehaved by running too much about the lodge, going thoughtlessly into the sacred place and making a noise in the presence of visitors, the mother did not beat it, but dashed cold water over its head, and if that had not the desired effect it was repeated. Then the child usually "had good ears," and sat down quietly.* Volume IV, page 26.

MNÁSHWAI – WISHHAM, 1910

*In primitive times the summer dress for both sexes was a small breech-cloth, and in winter the body was protected by a skin or a woven blanket obtained in trade. The region of the Dalles was a great trading centre, and naturally the people quickly acquired alien customs. Thus they very early adopted the plains manner of dress. Tattooing, head-flattening, and the wearing of a dentalium shell in the nasal septum were common to both sexes.* Volume VIII, page 172.

## "THE CHIEF HAD A BEAUTIFUL DAUGHTER," 1908

*"In the long, long ago, the chief had a very beautiful daughter. Long and brown like corn-silk was her glossy hair, so they called her Apísh. [The name Corn-silk proves the tale to be either a relic of an earlier agricultural life with their former brethren, the Hidatsa, or else a myth borrowed bodily from the lore of that tribe.] Handsome young men, brave warriors and good hunters, wooed her, but she gave them no encouragement. Neither the greatest deeds in battle nor lavish bestowal of presents could soften her heart."* Corn-silk and the Seven Stars, Volume IV, page 117.

(OPPOSITE)

## WOMAN AND CHILD – NUNIVAK, 1928

*Children and adults alike of the Nunivak group are healthy, as a rule, and exceptionally happy because they have been little affected by contact with civilization.* Folio plates 688, 694, Volume XX.

(OVERLEAF)

## WASHO CRADLE-BASKETS, 1924

*The designs on the sun-shades are phallic symbols. The separated diagonal lines indicate that the infant is male; the serrated line and the diamond pattern indicate female. The same symbolism appears on Paviotso cradle-baskets.* Volume XV, page 94.

## A CREE CAMP AT LAC LES ISLES, 1926

*A family group consisting of two middle-aged women, a young mother, and several children, camped at the lake while the rest of the band were haying in a swampy meadow some miles inland. They engaged in fishing with a gill-net and in gathering blueberries. In point of sanitation their tipi and their cooking methods left much to be desired.* Folio plate 628, Volume XVIII.

## KLAMATH CHILD, 1923

*The Klamath Indians of southeastern Oregon are the larger of two divisions of the Lutuami, the other being their neighbors, the Modoc.* Volume XIII, page 161.

## WISHHAM CHILD, 1909

*The Wishham. . . . are an inland extension of the Chinookan stock of the Pacific coast and the lower Columbia river – they are sedentary dwellers by the swift waters of the Columbia. In place of the horse, their means of travel was the picturesque high-prowed canoe common to the Pacific waters from the Columbia river to Yakutat bay in Alaska. They were a slave-holding community, possessing much pride of caste, and imbued with beliefs of magic to an unusual degree. Their myths possess a delightful wealth of imagination, and are all-embracing in their personification of the animal and the inanimate.* Volume VIII, page xii.

## A HOPI MOTHER, 1906

*The Hopi are without doubt among the most interesting of our surviving American Indians, and one of the very few groups recently living in a state similar to that of a hundred years ago. For the anthropologist the complexity of the ethnic elements that in the last three and a half centuries have combined to produce the modern Hopi, and the astonishing richness of their religious ceremonies, present a field crowded with opportunity. Artist and traveller are invariably entranced with the picturesque desert environment of the Hopi, with their ancient, many-storied, cliff-perched pueblos, their dramatic dances and artistic ceremonial costumes, their pleasing pottery and basketry, and no less pleasing manners.* Volume XII, page 3.

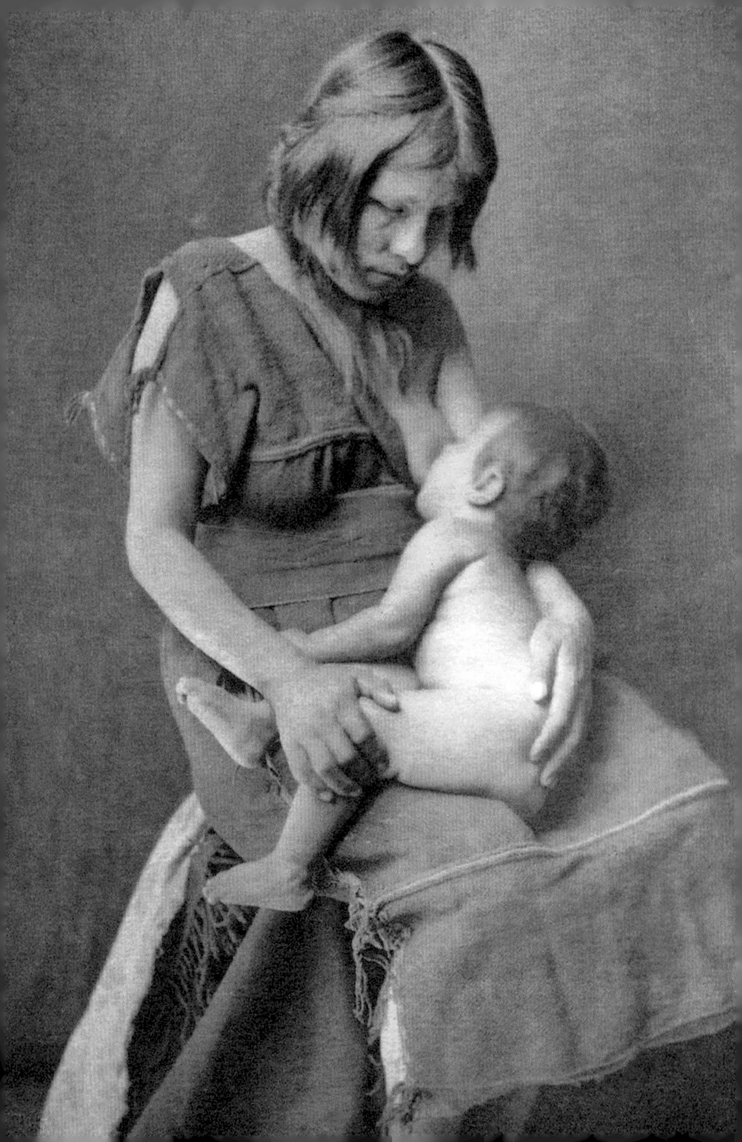

(OPPOSITE)

## AWAITING THE RETURN OF THE SNAKE RACERS – HOPI, 1921

*Chû-yûtu ("rattlesnake running") occurs on the last day of the ceremony. . . . The little boys on this morning are naked and painted white, and they have their hands full of cornstalks, melons, and other plants and fruits. As soon as the racers come in sight, the boys run about the mesa, while little girls pursue them and take away their plants and fruits. Thus is expressed the desire and the prayer that crops may grow rapidly.* Volume XII, page 150.

(OVERLEAF)

## HOMEWARD, 1898

*Working in wood was the most noteworthy industry practised by the Indians of the north Pacific coast, and many of its phases were peculiar to that region. With implements limited in variety and utterly primitive in design and material, they felled giant yellow cedars, which they burned and hewed into seaworthy canoes. . . .*

*Canoes of various sizes and designs are used by all the tribes, from the tiny, blunt-nosed river craft capable of carrying, somewhat precariously, two passengers, to that great seaworthy vessel accommodating twenty to thirty persons besides a considerable cargo of household utensils and food.* Volume IX, page 59.

## OKÚWA-TSIRE ("CLOUD BIRD") – SAN ILDEFONSO, 1905

*San Ildefonso is near the east bank of the Rio Grande, seven miles below San Juan and eighteen northwest of Santa Fe. . . .*

*The names of fifty-eight so-called clans have been recorded at San Ildefonso, of which seventeen were still represented in 1924. These are nominally divided into two ceremonial moieties, but members of the same clan may be found in both the larger divisions. These "clans" are patrilineal and not exogamous. . . .*

*The two ceremonial moieties are respectively Pá*$^n$*yo-tówa ("summer people"), or Pá*$^n$*yo-gerí́i*$^n$*-tówa, and Ténu*$^n$*rí́i*$^n$*-tówa ("wịnter [plural] people").* Volume XVII, pages 30, 39.

## APSAROKE MOTHER, 1908

*As descent is traced through the mother, her relatives are regarded with a feeling of the deepest respect. Particularly is the case with a mother's sisters, who are addressed as "mother," and to whom is manifested the same respect and sanctity one has for the natural mother. . . .*

*On the fourth day after the birth of a child a man of prominence, or in some instances a woman, was called in to bestow a name, which, as a rule, was one that he had heard called among the spirit-people in one of his visions, or perhaps one referring to some great deed of his own. Incense was made, and the child raised four times in the cloud of smoke to symbolize the wish that it might grow tall and vigorous.* Volume IV, pages 23, 25.

AN APACHE BABE, 1903

*A fortunate child picture, giving a good idea of the happy disposition of Indian children, and at the same time showing the baby carrier or holder.* Folio plate 17, Volume I.

THE DRINK – FLATHEAD, 1910

*Primarily they were fish-eaters, but parties of the Flatheads, Pen d'Oreilles, and Kalispel made annual journeys to the buffalo plains. . . . Deer and other mountain game were abundant, and roots and berries, especially camas, kouse, choke-cherries, and buckleberries, were staples.* Volume VII, page 163.

(OPPOSITE)

## QUILCENE BOY, 1912

*The Quilcene, like the Skokomish, are a band of Twana living on Hoods canal, Washington.* Folio plate 303, Volume IX.

(OVERLEAF)

## MOVING CAMP – ATSINA, 1908

*With the close of their buffalo-hunting days the Atsina have settled down in the foothills of the Little Rockies. . . . They were essentially a hunting people, raising no crops of any sort, and subsisting principally on the flesh of the buffalo. . . .Their dwelling was the buffalo-skin tipi. . . . Before horses were acquired, perhaps in the early years of the nineteenth century, the dog-travois was the means of conveyance; later, vehicles of the same kind, only larger, were drawn by horses. . . . The clothing of the men consisted of moccasins, hip-length leggings, loin-cloth, and, about the shoulders, a buffalo-robe as the weather demanded, or a shirt when the occasion justified gala garments; while the women were clad in moccasins, knee-length leggings, the one-piece dress falling from the shoulders to mid-calf, and in severe weather the buffalo-robe. Save the robe, all these garments were made of deerskin, or, excepting the woman's dress, of weathered buffalo-skin, and all were ornamented more or less with dyed porcupine-quill embroidery.* Volume V, pages 111-112.

## DAUGHTERS OF A CHIEF, 1907

*The dress of the women consisted of a garment made of finely tanned deerskins, which extended from the shoulders to midway of the knee and ankle. Sleeves reaching nearly to the wrist were tied at intervals on the under side. . . . A dress regarded as well-made was fringed at its bottom and sleeves, and finely decorated at the shoulders and arms with porcupine quills, beads, and shells. . . .*

*Leggings extending from knee to foot were worn by the women, and moccasins, ankle-high, usually also beautifully worked with quills and beads. . . . The hair was parted at the middle from front to back and arranged in two long braids, hanging in front of the shoulders and tied at the ends with a thong and ornaments.* Volume III, pages 28-29.